The Impossible Toystore

Also by Mark Perlberg

The Burning Field
The Feel of the Sun

The Impossible Toystore

poems

Mark Perlberg

Louisiana State University Press ❋ Baton Rouge MM

PS
3566
.E6915
I47
2000

Designer: Amanda McDonald Scallan
Typeface: Bembo
Typesetter: Coghill Composition
Printer and binder: Thomson-Shore, Inc.

Library of Congress Cataloging-in-Publication Data
Perlberg, Mark, 1929–
    The impossible toystore : poems / Mark Perlberg.
    p.   cm.
    ISBN 0-8071-2614-4 (alk. paper)—ISBN 0-8071-2615-2 (pbk. : alk. paper)
    I. Title.

    PS3566.E6915   I47   2000
    811'.54—dc21
                                                                00-028727

The author would like to thank the editors of the following journals, in which some of
these poems were first published, sometimes in slightly different form: *Hudson Review:* "The
Color of the Spirit," "The Floating World," "The Last News from *Voyager,*" "Summer,"
"What Happened in the Woods"; *Illinois Review:* "Cartography," *"Self-Portrait:* Camille
Pissarro"; *Images:* "Maybe It Will Stir," *"Portrait of a Boy,"* "Spaces"; *Midstream:* "Kabbala";
New Outlook, "Alchemy," "At a Holocaust Museum, Prague"; *Northeast Corridor:* "The
Connubial Wrens"; *Oyez:* "The Abandoned City"; *Poetry:* *"Garden Vision";* *Poetry East:*
"Geode"; *Prairie Schooner:* "Christina's Angel," "The Edge of the Forest," "The End of the
Holidays," "Ivar," "The Last Meeting," "Nightsweat," "The Passion of Vermeer," "The
Thought Garden," "Up in Maine"; *Willow Review:* "Love Letters," "Return to the Island."
    "A Question from Telemachus" originally appeared *The Great Ideas Today* (Ency-
clopaedia Britannica: Chicago, 1984).

For Anna
and for Michael, Joshua,
Alex and Ryan

Contents

One

In the Theater of Memory

Ivar

My grandfather Ivar, a Jew from Sweden,
landed in New York at twenty-three in the 1880s,
and met his wife-to-be in a boarding house in Brooklyn.
His family was jeweler to the king—so Mother said.
He was traveling the world to cure his migraine,
stopped in New York, married, and lived unhappily ever after.
Couldn't earn a living. So rich his family was
he wasn't trained for anything. So we were told.
Fathered four kids, fussed and grew old
in genteel poverty. Taught his daughters,
in this unruly land, opera tunes hummed on a pocket comb
covered with wax paper. A blue-eyed austere man
with a frosty beard and knickers like Bernard Shaw.
We saw him most on summer holidays.
He walked with a cane, wore sweaters even in the heat,
puffed from the back of his throat like a small
rhythmical engine, read the pulps by the yard,
Astounding Stories, Amazing Science Fiction,
despite knowledge of a half-dozen languages, even Aramaic.
So Mother said. Once or twice each summer he took
his cap and stick and walked down front to the firehouse
to beat the firemen at checkers.
They played outdoors under shade trees.

There was a story like a dark northern legend
Mother told about Ivar,
always with an odd throb of pride
in her voice: Once, his mother, Henrietta,
sent steamship tickets for the family to visit Sweden.
What did Ivar do?
Made a ticket pyre in a dish on the kitchen table,
wouldn't talk for days and scarcely ate.
His ice-blue eyes were filmed with—was it rage?
Who was Ivar? The black sheep of his family?
A dispossessed second son? Had he committed a crime

over the water, in Sweden? Did such thoughts
ever occur to Mother, who never failed to speak
of that hard Edwardian gentleman with reverence,
even love, despite the harsh story of her youth?
Which one of us will ever know the truth about Ivar,
who called my brother Sonny, seemed to dislike my sister,
lived on handouts from my father, and died when I was ten?

S u m m e r

I am watching the gardener trim our lawn. He pushes a mower
with a wooden handle over the grass, making dark stripes where
he cuts. The blades purr, sending up a little stream of green
as he pushes and pulls the mower forward and back. The green
arc sprays into a canvas grass catcher hooked to the mower's
wheels. I sit on the steps and tease a beetle with a blade
of grass as it moves up the slate walk. On the long summer days
between the times when the gardener comes with his truck and
his men to trim and edge the lawn and cut the long hedges, I
cut the grass, pushing our wooden mower. Or maybe I only dream
it, because I am very young and the sweet grass smell engenders
dreams. I water the lawn with the long rubber hose, sending
a fine buzz of water tickling down my arm, dripping on my sneakers.
Each day is stretched, is strangely long, and when the sun presses
on the tops of the trees at the edge of town, it floods the lawn
with the clearest watery light. Mother talks with someone on the
porch. Their voices blend with the purr of the mower and the
hiss of the water. The house is cool and airy. The winter
rugs and drapes and bedspreads have been taken up and stored in
the attic. The chairs wear cool summer coverings that are crisp
and shine a little in the afternoon light. We still live in the
big brick house at the head of the street. Father hasn't died yet.

In the Theater of Memory

I think of the time I entered
the toy shop with you
on an afternoon gray with the threat of rain.
Or do I recall images of you reminiscing,
recounting the story you loved to tell
of your small stepson-to-be
standing mute before racks, tables,
shelves of toys?

You would have purchased any of them
for me—lead soldiers firing muskets,
a mountain tunnel for my trains,
even a magic cape sewn with planets and stars,
but I never pulled my hands
from my pockets.

What I recall clearly is the way
you shook your head with mirthless laughter
each time you told the story down the years
of the strange boy who turned his back
on a hundred toys.

Only months before we entered the impossible
toystore, my father quit the family
by performing the unfathomable trick of dying.
Surely, he could have reversed the magic
that engrossed him as he lay on his bed
in the darkened room.
Surely, he could have turned the key
in the lock of himself and slipped the chains
he chose to wear, like Houdini,
another prince of the time.

Was not the story you never tired of telling
a slant account of a vexed and baffled boy

who would not forgive his father for disappearing,
nor you your entrance on the scene?

For I had seen him glide from our home
on a June evening,
saw him lift his straw boater in the air,
flash his broad Franklin Roosevelt smile,
then turn and vault the hedge
at the border of the lawn.

His heels made sidewalk music
down the street.

Up in Maine

Mother drew me toward her
on the lawn, kneeled
and took my hand.
"You must call Harry—Father—now.
Will you do that for me?"

I pulled my hand from hers
and walked away.

I see her kneeling on the grass,
white arms at her sides.
She turns and looks
out toward the bay.

Coda

for my mother

When I was six or seven
you stopped singing
as you moved about the house
as you dressed for evening

I'll see you again whenever
spring breaks through again
Time will lie heavy between

Remember the night

You played the piano
a piece with vivid Spanish
figures

I recall the fringed peach shawl
on the polished mahogany
When did you learn to play
you must have spent hours practicing
Why did you stop singing

If I had thought to ask
these questions when I was older
could you have found a way
to answer

The Edge of the Forest

Like the witch in a fairy tale,
she opened the kitchen door
and shoved her small son and daughter
out on the back stoop.
The lock sprang shut behind them.
She turned and walked away
deep inside the house.

It was a chill winter dusk,
the cobalt-blue sky
unstained by any cloud.
Limbs and fingers of trees
twisted across it.

In a swamp of rage and fear,
the boy punched his fist
through the glass
and opened the kitchen door,
saving himself and his sister
from the cuttlefish dark.

Confused, angry, loving,
she took the boy to the sink
amid the noise and crying
and teased needles of glass
from his hand.

The blood on that white door
is a sign on his doorpost still,
and the chill of that clear sky
a sliver in his heart.

A Question from Telemachus

We have the whole story from the bard,
but now that Father's and Mother's white bones
have been reduced to ash, prayer,
and blue plumes of smoke—between us,
he exaggerated a touch; "Old Knife,"
"Master of Land Ways and Sea Ways," "Great Tactician. . . ."

I'm sure it's true—what Father said
of those ten years
that ended in a hurricane of blood
in the great hall—
but what if he'd never come home?
What if his bones rolled
on the floor of an unnamed ocean cave?
Would I have taken on the suitors, finally,
broken them all?
Could I have sent the hornet death winging
across the bright hall, swarm after swarm
in a dark singing?

I'm king of this rocky island.
Commerce is sound. Between the stony outcrops
the fields are burnished with grain.
Blue grapes glitter in the arbors.
Even the arts flourish a little.

Yet sometimes in dreams I stand before the suitors
in the timbered hall,
heft the great bow from its niche in the wall,
string it easily as a girl ties a ribbon
in her hair,
slam an arrow against the shaft—
I wake before the first arrow
screams across air.

Family Pictures

1
It is autumn 1940.
Mom is driving our blue Chevrolet.
We are rolling up 9W, on the Jersey
side of the Hudson. Families drove
for pleasure then, in heavy roomy cars
down gray macadam roads.
Our destination, The Sylvan Tavern
on the great mesa of the Palisades.
We turn off the road, crunching gravel.
Harry, my sister and I wait in the car
for Mother. She returns with garlicky
hot dogs—each so juicy and packed,
the first bite makes a popping sound—
and dark, rich smelling coffee.

A day of peace in the family.
Mother hasn't sharpened her voice
on some invisible stone.
Harry content with himself,
not sunk in his chair,
coughing and snapping his paper.

2
An earlier, ghostly drive
unwinds like a half-lit film.
Our father is still alive. He grasps
the black wheel and seems in command,
but death rides in the gray Caddy
with the high roof and the oval
window in back.

3
Loud dinners in the apartment.
The turkey glows on the table.

Harry carves, his ring catching light
from the chandelier. More likely, Mother
attacks the great bird, brings it out
from the kitchen. My aunts follow
with steamy bowls of yams, beans
and woody mushrooms, fragrant thick-crusted
bread and mounds of cranberry sauce.

Pinochle after Sunday dinners. Harry and a pair
of uncles vie through the long afternoons,
laying each card down with a flourish,
a wisecrack and a snap.
Scarves of blue cigar smoke in the air.

4

Nothing constant but good food and trouble.
There came a day when Harry,
dwarfed by the baggage he held,
found my sister and me in the street.
He'd be away for a while. Couldn't
say how long. He'd keep in touch.

5

There came a time when I left their city
on the old Lackawanna Railroad.
Its smoke darkened the Hudson Valley
as I made my faltering way.

Bloodlines

On the back of an old photograph of you
I found four words you wrote;
they noted merely place and time.

Mother, that sudden token of your writing—
angular pitch of urgent, sloping letters—
blew wide the door to the country
we loved and warred in. Your sign.
Solid as a thumbprint, a gene map.
Never to appear anywhere in the world
again.

The Last Meeting

The last time I saw Harry alive—
I was leaving for home in another city—
he settled in his chair with his paper,
a man with something important to say.
He began with his trip to France in the twenties.
His cabbie drove up the hill of Montmartre,
swept his hand over the scene below: "Monsieur—Paris."
The gesture meant something to Harry.
It had stayed with him fifty years.

"There should be places here like they have
over there, where people like you could meet
with friends and over a glass or two of wine,
talk half the night of important things."

He never said any such thing before. It meant,
though your road will be different from mine,
here is my blessing.

Two

Nightsweat

What Happened in the Woods

I scarcely think the boys invented it all—
it's such a complicated story.
They were biking home after a movie
on the path that angles through the forest preserve—
it parallels the main street in town, a few blocks west—
when Kevin skidded into the grass to avoid
what might have been a shadow or a hole.
A wood turtle, big as a soup bowl, stared up at the boys,
its head way out of its leathery shell.
As they kneeled to examine the creature,
up through a grove of alder on the river side of the path
a figure of mist rose, gathered in the rough shape of a man,
though you couldn't tell if it was man or woman—
but it was no way human.
Think of a cowl, a robe of mist.
It crossed the path and lingered beside the bikes
resting against some trees.
The boys froze. They stood opposite,
naked as fingers held to test the wind,
but there was no wind
or any rag or scrap of mist rising off the river.
They dropped down in a grove of birches.
Above, a pair of dark birds circled.
Soon, the leaves of the trees nearby
stood erect in the air,
and a second figure of mist
drifted from the river toward the bikes.
Overhead, the birds kept turning, turning.
After a time the pair—tuned to what design?—
moved back across the path in a kind of waver
and melted into some trees.
The boys sprang on their bikes—
there were still two hours of daylight—
and fled like a single bowshot,

but not before my Kevin marked the spot
with a crumpled beer can.

A year—to the day—after the boys saw
whatever it was they saw,
a pair of girls was murdered in the woods.
Where they lay, canceled, discarded, strewn among leaves
near the river,
someone, something, had hung a can
all rusted over.
It swung from a branch by a muddy twist
of rope.

Geode

I had a friend who imperceptibly
became my bitter foe.
I don't know which the more painful,
the poison drop by drop,
or the shock of the turning
that grew unknown to him or me
like crystal teeth inside a stone.

Nightsweat

The poem I need to write is the poem of rage.
Not the poem of sinking into harmony with wind rhythms,
wave sounds lapping this northern island.
Nor the poem of the round of seasons, effulgent summer
dying into fall. Nor of taking my place
in the cycle of generations.

I need to write how the great wind came on a filthy night,
rammed up the coast, ripped spruce eighty feet tall
and strewed them like straw over a neighbor's
woodlot, a man who built his house deep in those woods
and painted it black.

I need to write of the squire on the crest of my hill,
who left a trail of stumps and ash from his house
clear down to the bay, trashing a woman's land
because her treetops smudged his view of sunsets,
clouds, boats passing.

How my daughters, both, were given
halting, difficult sons.
Of their nightsweats, vigils, sorrows.
But most—how the surgeon split my chest
with a whirling saw and took out my heart.

O blooming world of chaos and decay,
I want my old heart back, not this alien pump
that was pressed, cut, chilled, changed,
and held in hands remote from me
as those of a man on a spacewalk, working
with delicate instruments
in the violent dark.

Cartography

Taking soap, cloth, and clear water
to an anonymous old oil—five trees in a dun landscape—
I rinse grime away. Color gradations pulse.
A man in a tall white hat steps from behind
a tree. Black jacket, leggings, breeches.
He seems to know me and appears just as I begin
a journey to a land whose maps glare
with empty spaces, roads narrow into trails
that vanish, and the patterned stars change
their configurations.

I look away from the picture.
Nothing in the room has changed,
or in the weather. The brilliant day
flows on. He signals with his walking stick.
We meet at the edge of seeing.

Garden Vision

after the painting by Paul Klee

It is a soft night on the streets of my city
with gold October burning in the air.
The sky is palpable, smoky,
remote from the glass-hard sky of winter.
We have been given Rilke's two more golden days.
It is time to wander after work under rustling leaves,
saffron streetlights, toward my autumn garden.
It will appear at a turn of some unlikely street.
Maybe there will be a stream, beyond a patch of thistles,
patterned with leaves,
a stone path worn smooth by desire,
a shell of a tower, each brick burning within
like the yellow flares of the leaves,
a sun dial, its blade sheathed in the dark,
a pumpkin moon glowing like a heart,
and at the far end of my garden,
a wall etched with signals and runes
that will tremble as I read them
into meaning.

Self-Portrait: Camille Pissarro

He stares at me like my conscience,
looming before a window open on a street
in Paris. His life is almost over.
He says: This is who I am.

All is dark and silvery. The fall
of his beard, light glinting on a rim
of his half-glasses. The window silvery behind him.
He says: The world doesn't flow in circus colors.
That vision isn't serious. It moves in plainer
shades: browns, greens, cloud colors,
and this buoyant, silvery light of Paris.

He says: I prefer what happens again and again.
Peasants in a row mowing. Patterns of movement
on the boulevards, shifting yet the same.
A farm girl in a violet dress,
head awkwardly bent, musing over her bowl of coffee.

Alchemy

Kafka lived in this small blue house
that teeters and leans on Alchemy Street,
where Emperor Rudolph installed scholars
to coax tin into gold. It's just a shout
from the castle of a thousand rooms.

"I'll ennoble the man who brews gold in a pot,"
the emperor said.

"The castle," said Kafka, "that we see
from every point in Golden Prague
is a swarm of shadows. It isn't there.
I've tested its reality with alchemical
instruments of my own. It's built
entirely, stone on stone, of air."

Kabbala

Prague is erasing itself.
Stucco falls from sand-colored palaces.
Black scaffolding climbs the spiky towers of Saint Tyn,
grows greasy with disuse in rain.
In the night an old Jew dreams the Grand Rabbi
has forgotten all the secret names of God.

At a Holocaust Museum, Prague

In the photomural a boy of twelve looms
in a crowd beside the transports.
He wears a sweater buttoned to the throat
against the chill, hefts a suitcase
as though leaving with his family on a holiday.
Big shoulders, chest, hair fresh-cut,
alert strong face that fell to ash,
melted in smoke, in ropes and sheets of snow
flying over Poland.
Decades later, in another country,
my brother wore that face.

The Jewish Cemetery at Olšany*

No one comes to cut the grass at Olšany,
to pull weeds from the dark graves
of Rosenzweigs, Lippmans, Mandelbaums,
who died in their beds before the last pogrom.
There are no Jews in Prague anymore;
the graves are drowning.
Wild rivers of ivy, myrtle, everlasting,
flash in June lightning against the tombs.

*pronounced "Ohlshany"

The Abandoned City

The great buildings stand empty in the sunlight. Not a face
is seen at a window, inside a shop. Doors hang open; signs
creak in wind. The old-fashioned cars with their soft,
feminine lines are parked in neat rows along the curbs. No one
approaches them, opens a door, slides behind the dashboard,
drives away. If there is an enemy, he has not shown himself;
his appearance would bring a kind of relief. For weeks a column
of oily smoke has been rising in the Tular district. We do not
know how the fire started or why it burns with such a hard green
light. Someone saw a horse walking down the center of the
Avenue of Heroes. It must have wandered in from the city's
edge, like the crowlike birds that have clamped themselves to
the aerials of all but the tallest buildings. At the airport,
saber grass grows in cracks along the runways. No one in our
family recalls an order demanding that anyone leave.
We have been faithful and have nothing to fear.

Maybe It Will Stir

He moves now at the edges of the world
in windy margins where sleet spills into rain,
where the sea flows into the mouths of northern rivers.
He listens for what might be in wind-ripples, indications,
watching how dusk, issuing its purple,
takes a far-off hill.
He's grown used to fingering silence,
like a merchant his coin.
Maybe it will stir in the shadow of stones,
in a trumpet note of light glancing off a wave.

The Last News from *Voyager*

When the craft was about to fling beyond
the tidal haul of the nine planets
and fall toward the hives of stars,
they turned the cameras around
and took a few snapshots of home:
A blue drop shining. A tear.

Three

The Floating World

The Thought Garden

I will build a thought garden behind my house.
Raked sand or gravel flowing will stand
for a stream, the sea, or trackless woods.
Gnarled rocks anchored in twos, threes,
will be mountains, islands, plunging cliffs,
or clusters of friends—the Poets of the Bamboo Grove,
perhaps—who made boats of their poems
and floated them out on the river.
There will be no bright colors in my garden.
Evergreens, rather, or moss that has no skin to shed,
for we are talking not of evanescent things
but of the bones and marrow of the world.

The Color of the Spirit

The cranes fly across the gray-green bowl,
three cranes with legs stretched out behind them,
wearing red crowns. They fly above the crackle
of the glaze, twists of clouds.
It would be too simple to say the bowl is the color
of jade, as the old Chinese poets often put it:
Though we are cleft by exile, my love,
we gaze tonight at the same jade moon.
Rather, it is a pond widening into a lake
opening into a river still brushed by mist.
It is a little sea in my hands. Serene.

The Floating World

for Anna

1

Sounds of koto and flute spool from the radio
this January morning.
Thirty years ago we were in Japan.

2

Fuji's snow-cone, flushed in early light,
soared above the gate at the edge of the garden,
as though we'd borrowed the holy mountain—
visible from a hundred miles away
only in clearest air of winter—for the morning.
When we rose my shirt was so cold you thawed
it at the stove. I left the house,
turned a corner
and the mountain disappeared.

3

Blowing curtains in the wine shops.
Fire in the waxed-paper lanterns
red as blood.

4

Returned to our room in the 300-year-old inn,
its walls, sliding doors, brown as oak leaves.
In the light of the floor lamp, our futon spread
to receive us was the color of moss in noon sunlight.
Rain brushed the city, dripped
from the evergreens, the stone lantern
in our private garden.

5

You sang lieder with our student-guide in Kyoto
eight years after Hiroshima.
Temples, palaces, a walled sand garden.
Back home, I failed to answer his letter.

6

These scenes from the beginning of our story
shine like slides on a white wall.
I reach for them, give them the permanence
of thin lines of ink on ruled paper.
They can matter only to you and me.

Love Letters

Our letters you packed so long ago
in the transparent plastic box—
Plastics were new then.
The box seemed quaint a decade later
when plastics no simple saw could cut
or fire burn entered all our lives.
You tied our letters into packets,
dropped them into the brittle case
that had, itself, to be tied with string.

The many times I said, "Burn the letters.
Feed them to some small, inconsequential flame."
Too late, after the crash that took us
like a pair of storm-smashed birds.

I didn't want our children rummaging in our letters.
The things we told each other—sundered
by the usual, useless war! I didn't want them
reading wild words about the meadow your body
was to me. Its shoreless stream.

Burn the letters? As usual you were wiser.
They will sift through them one by one.
Children, we were shameless.
Flameless the fire in which we burned.

Doors (Prague)

Three violins molded in stucco
above a door on Neruda Street.

Pale green door to the Tyl where Mozart
first led *Don Giovanni*.

A vast wood door hammered with spikes
of iron studs.

Ten thousand doors through which Jews flowed
toward the chimneys.

Iron flowers, frosted glass—
the door you'll never walk through again.

Half a World

At the zoo in a microsecond
you were left
with a single good green eye.
Quick as a bird passing
a shadow bloomed
deep behind the lens
of the other.

Now I wake before dawn and listen
for your small night noises.

Should we imagine our world halved
by the absence of the other—
a form of inoculation—like the king
who supped each day on a drop of poison
and died old?

Your Winter Coat

Remember that winter coat
I was so fond of?
We picked it out together
at the beginning of our story.
Threads of Isfahan red close-woven
with nubby strands of black. Silk-soft.
I loved helping you unbutton
its long row of small black buttons
when you came in from the cold.

Last night it shone
like a Persian carpet in a sunny room.
I woke with tears on my face.

Out There

The Chinese painters didn't use
a vanishing point to show perspective.
   Washes of light and lighter color
   indicated distances—past cliffs, streams
   and humped bridges, past water falling
   from the lip of a rock into a gorge,
   out to farthest pales and shallows,
   where the Immortals ride great fishes and turtles,
   sporting in the unseen world.

Return to the Island
after Wang Wei

I've come home to our northern island,
letting go thoughts of who is in or out.
The white morning sun climbs above
our cottage, dispelling dawn's chill,
rousing thrushes, wrens, waxwings
that dart to our trees and bushes.
I love their chatter and song,
their quick flight, their perfect bodies
and how branches bend or spring up
as they leave or light.
I cook eggs and boil water for tea.
You ask what laws rule failure or success?
Shouts of children in the orchard
raise a scatter of birds.

The Connubial Wrens

Yes to the golden moment that is gold
a moment only in the cramped dirt garden
in our backyard. Yes to the tottering wall,
the blunt back porches of anonymous neighbors,
the toys abandoned on flagstones—
yellow tractor, dump truck, chunky cement mixer.
Yes to the crows in their baseball umpire suits
on the telephone wires, to the connubial wrens
hunkering in the Chinese elm, its leaves still green.
Yes to the black squirrel eyeing me
from the gate, the herbs in their pots,
sage, thyme, sweet marjoram,
the jet flashing this instant overhead.

The Passion of Vermeer

Whether a servant girl is pouring cream into a bowl,
or a young woman, elegant in satin, glances
in a mirror at her knight as she plays the clavier;
whether the turbaned girl, grown famous
these three hundred years, looks suddenly back
at the viewer, lips parted,
the subject of the painter was time—
seized by fixing what is most fleeting.

That is how it was, you say, and is,
as your wife plays an old tune on the piano,
as sunlight streams across your desk,
striking the road atlas open for a trip
and the photo of your son balancing
on one leg beside a gate, smiling.

On a Photograph of a Headless Greek Statue in the Living Room of a Friend

1

The nose is usually first to disappear,
smashed by some vandal with a rock or hammer.
If the figure is a woman, the prominent breast
is scarred. Centuries of wind, rain,
polluted air.
Anything that protrudes is vulnerable,
a penis, arms, but here the head is gone,
and she leans, propped against fallen columns,
ambiguous as history.

2

Now that all is over with Martha,
each photo from her collection
but this one is tagged with the name of an heir.
I want to claim this photograph
for remembrance. Why?
I have no answer. Because
I imagine intelligent oval eyes
and hair bound in the Attic way.
Because her draped body is fine, relaxed,
elegantly female.
Because of her proven vulnerability
or the way she leans gently backward
with time washing over her in this quiet place.
Because I remember the apposite Shelley poem.

3

It is early October, the weather still hot,
the air spiked with the scent of eucalyptus.
The Aegean sparkles beyond the burnt hills.
Below, rows of olive trees flash silver and black.

She takes joy, deep-dyed as Tyrian purple, in all this,
and walks, arms upraised, smiling, to meet a friend
who appears—just now—on the path
at the far edge of the field, waving
and calling out her name.

Four

From the Deep Kitchen

Christina's Angel

There in the island cemetery—
you know the kind,
a few graves bunched together
out of the wind—
was the fresh grave of a child.
What caught my eye
was the painted plaster angel
at the head of the mound.
She held a banner where
I read the child's name.
What I can't forget
is the toy bear set down at the grave.
Its fur had begun to ravel in the weather.
Had a small sister or brother
brought the bear to this place,
or had the parents crossed a border
of some kind and there
summoned an apposite angel
against the dark, the owls' hooting,
the coming rains?

Some Questions about a Ghost

"You the one who bought the farm off the highroad?
Nobody told you the place is haunted?"
The druggist in the village gave me a look.
"They say the woman appears in an upper room,
staring out a window."

I said I hadn't much time for spirits.
Been a builder most of my life—
roads, houses. Worked on all the turnpike
bridges, Portland to Augusta.

Not a week after we settled in, I saw her.
Around midnight. She stood with her back to the bed,
a woman in a gown, peering out toward the road.
I thought it was Harriet, but Harriet lay asleep
on the moonlit side of the bed.

Couldn't see her face. Wish I had. I've imagined
a thousand times a fox's snout, red eyes flaring.
She turned, walked right past me
and vanished like breath on a mirror.
I never told Harriet.

Soon after, when Harriet was putting up paper
in that room, she felt a chill
and smelled a scent like cloves.
The paper she had rolled out on the wall
slid to the floor. Then another and
another.

"Listen here," Harriet snapped. "Listen here.
Robert and I own this place now.
I've put in time fixing up this room
and I intend to finish."

Harriet got on with the job.
The paper stayed up on the wall
and has ever since. That was the last
we heard from the ghost
while we lived at the farm.

Had she found what she was looking for
out there in the dark?
Was she as scared of me as I was of her?
One thing more:
Why wasn't Harriet frightened?

Letter to Huckleberry Finn

We said there weren't no place like a raft after all.
Other places do seem so cramped and smothery.

I thought of you again today, anchored
in the lee of a river island,
heard the oar-slap, the brown water
lapping the edges of your raft,
and I entered my own echoing summer
when I swam in quiet coves,
fished for cunner and pollock
over the side of a yellow punt,
made way with my older brother,
riding green swells, to grim Ram Island Light.

We returned summer after summer.
Three days it took driving New York to Portland
till we wound through the brick streets
of the old city
and ferried over to the island.

We eased out of the harbor, past
the breakwater with its odd potbelly light,
chugged past the Civil War fort
that rose out of the bay,
past the Diamonds, with their green crowns
and cliffs of rusted iron,
and made fast at Forest City Landing.

Up the cobbled street we rode
in the packed Chevy, in and out of glare
and morning shadow. How alive everything was—
the houses with great porches above the bay,
their Fourth of July parades of garden flowers,
flags of laundry flapping.

We turned east at Weber's Store
toward our cottage on the ocean side

of the island. Then, uphill,
around a bend, past the icehouse
that sagged in a swamp, down a tunnel
of scrub pines and leaning telephone poles—
the first blue shout of open sea.
I was home again, Huck, for one more summer.
Safe, free on my raft.

Portrait of a Boy

after Odilon Redon

You stare out of the portrait,
a brilliant boy in a blue sweater
Mama chose to match your wide-set eyes,
but your gaze is inward, is shadowed.
You think: She packed me off to bed
without supper, after the quarrel with Odette:
Sister is a coquette and a liar!
She smashed the vase on the solarium floor.
And you think: Sleek, poppy-tipped breasts
of the kitchen maid surprised after her bath.
What could she do but cry out softly, once,
then cover herself with her towel.
You turn away and dream: My time will come.
My name will sound in the high-arched future
like a crash of brass in a mossy garden.

Toward the Solstice

We burned our leaves on the bluest October day,
the sun still warm on our backs,
frost just a ghost in the shrubbery.
We raked the leaves into shifting piles on the lawn,
scooped them into deep round baskets
and spilled them in the street against the curb.
The vein of fire, unseen at first in diamond light,
whispered through oak leaves brown as butcher paper,
and maple still flushed with color like maps
torn from *The Book of Knowledge*.
We were letting go of October, relinquishing color,
readying ourselves for streets lacquered with ice,
the town closed like a walnut, locked inside the cold.

The Second Life of Christmas Trees

In frozen January, my friends and I
would drag discarded Christmas trees
from the sidewalks of our shivering town
to an empty lot. One match and fire
raced down a dry sprig like a spurt of life.
A puff of wind and the pile ignited,
flamed above our heads. Silk waves.
Spice of pitch and balsam in our nostrils.

We stood in a ring around the body of the fire—
drawn close as each boy dared,
our faces stinging from the heat and cold,
lash of that wild star burst on a winter night.

From the Deep Kitchen

Fill a large pot with cold water.
Add chunks of celery, parsley root
and the purple-tinged turnip.
When the vegetables soften,
slide the chicken into the pot.
When the bird is golden, add sprigs
of parsley and carrot circles.
The yellow broth will soothe you.
The meat steeped in the liquor
of root vegetables will sustain you.
This is a message from the deep kitchen
of childhood. Pass it on.

Pedagogy

My first-grade teacher, Pearl Lorraine Wright,
stood before her class, her hair a thin,
fleecy cloud.
"Children, it's not good for your eyes
to wear rubbers all day in school.
Put them in the cloakroom, please."
Even then I smiled behind my hand.

"Children, watch me. This is how to
open a new book without cracking
the spine."

I settle in my study, out of a whirling
storm, snap on the gooseneck lamp
and open a new book, *Dawn of Art:
Paintings from the Chauvet Cave,*
set the spine on the desk,
press the boards down and smooth out
the pages, a few at a time, half right,
half left, and think of Miss Wright,
in Palisade School Number 4
in a town that no longer exists.
Bisons, horses, rhinos, lions
march across the golden wall
of the cave—my snowboots neatly
placed in the hall closet.

The End of the Holidays

We drop you at O'Hare with your young husband,
two slim figures under paradoxical signs:
United and Departures. The season's perfect oxymoron.
Dawn is a rumor, the wind bites, but there are things
fathers still can do for daughters.
Off you go looking tired and New Wave
under the airport's aquarium lights,
with your Coleman cooler and new, long coat,
something to wear to the office and to parties
where down jackets are not de rigueur.
Last week winter bared its teeth.
I think of summer and how the veins in a leaf
come together and divide
come together and divide.
That's how it is with us now
as you fly west toward your thirties.
I set my new cap at a nautical angle, shift
baggage I know I'll carry with me always
to a nether hatch where it can do only small harm,
haul up fresh sail and point my craft
toward the punctual sunrise.

S p a c e s

Leave a space for the unexpected.
The red sun put out by fog at noon.

The tree backlit on our walk that night—
a vast face on the fog's scrim.

The adagio of Mahler's Fifth on the radio
when we came in, played not like a dirge
but a song.